TOWARD FREEDOM IN SINGING

Three Articles

Dina Soresi Winter
and
Theodora Richards

RSCP

9200 Fair Oaks Blvd.
Fair Oaks, California 95628

TABLE OF CONTENTS:

INTRODUCTION

Singing is a noble art. Nowadays, we are often reminded that it can hold the mirror up to nature. Many songs reflect the psychological pain and dissonance of our age, and many voices are trapped by materialism. However, singing can also express a special kind of freedom from physical bondage. Then it becomes a joyous, light-filled artform expressive of Humanity as it moves toward freedom.

The beauty of such singing is that it produces pure tones which are both exact and individual. It is a paradox worth noting that great singers bring a pristine exactitude *and* an individual quality as well. For many years I have heard Dina Soresi Winter achieve such qualities with Waldorf Institute choirs and with individual students. More recently her work with choirs in several places in Europe and the U.S.A. has demonstrated that remarkable levels of artistic performance can be reached along the lines indicated in this book.

Dina Winter is an artist-teacher continuing work begun by Gracia Ricardo* and her

---

*The American Grace Richards

i

niece, Theodora Richards. An American *Lieder* singer of international repute, Gracia Ricardo formulated her singing method with the help of Rudolf Steiner. She knew him well in Berlin and in Dornach and had many discussions with him. The article from the pen of her devoted successor, Theodora Richards, elucidates and elaborates upon the distinctive features of Madame Ricardo's singing method.

This book fulfills a need because it is a first indication of a path of singing in the light of Spiritual Science based on the insights gained by Gracia Ricardo and Theodora Richards.

Musicians interested in Anthroposophy will know that the work of Rudolf Steiner has also inspired other creative approaches. As an educator I find it a source of wonder and satisfaction to observe how different individuals of stature can become creative and can find new artistic disciplines for their art with the help of Spiritual Science.

To return to the work begun by Madame Ricardo and so ably represented by Dina Winter—I find it healing, delightful, and full of promise for the future.

Werner Glas, Ph.D.
July 1986

I. SPIRITUAL ASPECTS OF SINGING

"Singing, as a revelation of all that moves the innermost soul, is well one of the most joyful, one of the noblest ways of experiencing one's true self."

"On wings of song, through the gentle-sounding voice of the I within our souls, we are raised above the earthly and transitory, for pain and joy, happiness and suffering become objectified in our singing."

"Melody is the sounding mirror-image of man's thought and idea world."

Professor Friederich Oberkogler

Most modern training in singing is based upon methods which consider only the physical organism. Today, vocal methods often include the showing of charts to voice students as part of the lesson—charts indicating the organs connected with singing (larynx, tongue, soft palate, hard palate, diaphragm, etc.). These charts are used to demonstrate what happens, or is supposed to happen, to the vocal organs as one sings. They are meant to be a conscious aid in learning how to sing better.

1

I have known of several singers who initially had very good voices yet who emerged in complete desperation from these vocal studios, wondering if they would ever be able to sing again. Because they could not squeeze themselves into the fixed forms demanded of them by their teachers, they fled. Some sought their own paths and found the key which led them to their own individual singing freedom. Birgit Nilsson, the great Swedish soprano, is one of these. But not many can do this. Consequently, it often happens that singers who have been through a full university training which included such a mechanical approach can hardly produce a joyful tone again. The singing is tight, unfree, and certainly not a healing experience either for themselves or for their listeners. It would have been far better for these singers if they had not taken voice training at all! This is not to imply that there are not good singing teachers in the universities and in private studios. There are, although it is not a common occurrence to find one. Some teachers still have an intuitive, innate feeling for good singing and often use imaginative pictures and a fine sense of hearing to guide their gifted pupils.

In most of the accepted methods in teaching singing today, however, the prevailing thought is that the physical organs can be manipulated and controlled to produce tones. It is usually only the very gifted who instinctively know how to avoid the pitfalls of singing too mechanically. The artist in them often leads them to a more spiritual awareness of singing and keeps them from getting stuck in an approach which is purely physical. But, as these instincts forsake us more and more, we may well ask: "What will the future have in store for singing and its representatives?"

Grace Richards[1], an American singer in the early 1900's, asked this same question of Rudolf Steiner. He answered that singing is not a physical process. He said that the singer must be freed from a mechanical approach to singing and awakened to an understanding of true tone which is of a spiritual nature. Through such an understanding, based on knowledge of spiritual scientific principles, the singer can experience what Rudolf Steiner refers to as the "leading over of the tone into the etheric." ("*Überleiten des Tones ins Aetherische*"). Out of this, a new approach to singing arises wherein the singer will have an all-engrossing experience that his whole being is a resounding column of tone (*"eine klingende Saule"*). The entire etheric organization becomes involved in the singing process. One's whole being sings.

[1]While performing in Europe during the early part of the 20th century, she Italianized her name to Gracia Ricardo as was often done by professional singers of her day.

Rudolf Steiner is known to have said that Gracia Ricardo had the 'free tone.' Out of Rudolf Steiner's encouragement and numerous conversations with him, and through her study of many references to singing, to eurythmy and to music, found in his writings, she evolved an art of singing which leads the singer to an experience of the etheric activity in singing. Instead of beginning with physical functions, she started with tone based on the word, best begun with the help of a consonant. This gives the tone an acoustical shell, where all resonators can freely resound, thus revealing the full capacity of the voice.

The cultivation of a sense of hearing is an important part of this singing approach. Tone is carried through the air to our ears, but it is the etheric which carries the real essence of the tone to our inner being. Through an intensified listening, the outer tone is carried within, becomes an inner experience and greatly affects the tone one can then sing. Goethe once wrote in his *Tonlehre* (*"Theory of Tone"*): "One should pay particular attention to the leading of the tone inward through the ear, which acts in a thoroughly stimulating and productive way on the voice. The activity of the voice is thereby awakened, set in motion, enhanced and increased. The whole body is activated."

4

In Theodora Richards'[2] perceptive essay, *The Singer as Instrument* (Part II of this publication), she describes a path which may be followed by those seeking to develop the voice in a more conscious and healthy way. This essay offers an approach to finding one's own true tone. It offers the means whereby that tone can reflect the universal tone which streams around us. When we link ourselves to it in the right way, it flows and resounds through us.

Theodora Richards refers to the term, *Embouchure*, also used by wind instrumentalists as a proper start of the tone. She states that the *Embouchure* may be thought of as the starting and focal point for singing—an imaginary point on the lower lip where the inner air meets the outer. The *Embouchure* here described must take place in a comfortable range of the voice. There must be no vocal strain (demonstration by a teacher would be essential at the beginning). If this anchor for the voice is properly found, as the voice soars upward or downward, the tones find their own 'placement'—their own proper 'home' in and around us. The body becomes the firm yet flexible instrument which gives the proper physical basis for each emerging tone. As singers, our task then is to consciously *allow* the necessary processes to take place so that the tones can be born through us in a free

---

[2] the niece of Grace Richards

and healthy way. The whole body is activated from below the feet, so to speak, to above the head. The singer must find his inner and outer balance on each tone. Each tone must find its own balance in him.

Each rise or fall of the voice needs a new set of subtle inner adjustments which one cannot possibly control purely physically, any more than an archer can control each minute physical adjustment of his arm and hand when he draws his bow to shoot the arrow. But he can keep his eye on the goal and see to it that no rigidities prevent him from taking good aim. The ear is to the singer what the eye is to the archer. But the activity is more an inner one with the singer.

With the *Embouchure,* we have a means of leading the tone into that etheric realm of which Rudolf Steiner speaks. Moreover, the *Embouchure* provides the proper start of the tone by means of a word correctly enunciated on a given pitch. Once the tone is 'there' in an unforced but definite way, the other tones can follow on the same stream and a balanced inner mobility throughout the whole organism occurs, which, of course, must include a flexible action of the diaphragm based on proper breathing. A healthy stream of sound for the entire range of the voice can thus be achieved. In singing, there is movement. It is not just an outpouring of sound, but a balanced inner and outer streaming of tone which is connected with the universal tone.

Lamperti, the great Italian vocal master of the 19th century, had a feeling for this when he spoke of "drinking in the tone" (*"bere il suono"*). As already mentioned, we activate this universal tone within us when we sing correctly. It is as if beings were weaving in, out and around us in flowing movement when we sing.

We can be grateful to Theodora Richards for introducing to us her aunt, Gracia Ricardo's, comprehensive and rich views of singing based on anthroposophy. She has made her own significant contribution by further developing the understanding of this helpful technique of the *Embouchure*. (Italian schools of voice would refer to singing "on the lips" (*"sulle labbra"*) or singing "forward" (*"davanti"*) this "singing forward" is not to be understood in any way as "pushing" or forcing the tone outward, which could only be detrimental to the voice and to good singing) but Theodora Richards' explanation of the *Embouchure* makes understandable the original meaning of these terms in a way which is clear and useable for us today.

The *Embouchure* was mentioned in the yet unpublished manuscript by Gina Palermo and Hilda Deighton, both professional singers who studied for many years with Gracia

Ricardo after they had already achieved a certain degree of success in their field. In their manuscript, they describe the methods, techniques and basic premise of singing which they learned from Gracia Ricardo, who had achieved recognition as a concert singer in Europe and in the United States. As has been mentioned, Madame Ricardo had met Rudolf Steiner while she was in Europe and was greatly influenced by him and his work.

As a professional opera and concert singer, primarily in Europe, I had for a long time been searching for an approach to singing which would be based on an understanding of the human being in the light of Spiritual Science. I felt that the basic principles of such an approach would have to be applicable to the amateur as well as to the professional singer.

I had met a few teachers abroad who were working toward the realization of this goal and derived several helpful ideas from them. When I returned to the United States, I met Theodora Richards and, through her, the work of her aunt. This work was based on many years of experience in the field of singing. Founded on the work of Rudolf Steiner, it contained deep spiritual insights and seems to me a true basis for a school of singing. It offered that which I had long sought:

a practical training with a spiritual dimension and foundation.

This study hopes to give a few signposts along the way towards a freer singing. It is not meant to be a 'do-it-yourself-manual,' for no one can learn how to sing from a book. But, if a degree of freedom and good technique has already been achieved by a singer, he or she will be able to recognize and make use of sound vocal ideas, provided the open-mindedness is there. Such persons may be able to find in this some ideas with which to help themselves and others to a more conscious yet safe approach to singing.

No one method or approach to singing should be regarded as the *only* one. Gracia Ricardo herself was the first to admit that this approach should be regarded as "one of the ways" by which to achieve freedom in singing based on the spiritual scientific principles given to us by Rudolf Steiner. Healthy, sound approaches to singing will find meeting points with other approaches to singing. The dimension which is new is the spiritual-scientific view of Anthroposophy. On this basis, the old can be understood in a new way, and a conscious approach more appropriate to our day can become the basis for a new school of singing without in any way destroying the wisdom of the past.

In singing, we open ourselves to those forces which lift us above the every-day worlds. When we sing together, we meet each other on a deeper level than usual. Rightly experienced, singing links us with the etheric realm, with each other and with the spiritual source of tone itself.

My work with Theodora Richards, with the unpublished manuscript on singing by Hilda Deighton and Gina Palermo mentioned earlier, and with Rudolf Steiner's Anthroposophy, all form the basis of my approach to the teaching of singing with individuals and with student groups.

—Dina Soresi Winter

II. THE SINGER AS INSTRUMENT

The following brief essay is a supplement to an unfinished manuscript by Hilda Deighton and Gina Palermo. It will attempt to set forth some further thoughts on a new way of singing that, carefully guided and practiced, gradually allows the universal tone to sing through the singer.

Those who wish to link their song with the tone streaming through the world around them cannot remain just as they are. They must lift their mood to another level and cultivate receptive quiet and attentive listening. These qualities are basic to becoming an instrument for the world tone to play upon.

The sound each species of animal instinctively makes has its own distinctive tonal timbre. This allows but a partial inflowing of the universal tone. Tones may be conjured forth from all sorts of inanimate objects. But a human being must deliberately undergo a spiritual discipline to become, with his own unique timbre, a fuller, more complete and individualized instrument of this universal tone.

And this is what my aunt and teacher, Grace Richards, did. Prompted by her study of Anthroposophy and her personal conversations with Rudolf Steiner, she developed a new method of 'etheric' singing.

Her pupils were introduced to the concept of the evolution of tone. What had begun as the thinking of the gods later became motion, setting the planets moving along their paths. Modern space research has come upon certain sounds apparently proceeding from cosmic processes that Kepler described as the *Harmonia Mundi*. Later still, tone developed formative capacity. If we look attentively into the world, we see this mirrored all about us: the so-called Chladnian tone figures, produced by musical vibration, present striking examples of this. A great deal of reference material describing this evolution is available. Rudolf Steiner's lectures contain an infinitude of such information, and Guenther Wachsmuth's two volumes on the ethers also deal with it extensively.

The following steps that I have worked out are based on study with my aunt, Grace Richards. Instead of starting her pupils on the usual physical training emphasized by other methods, such as the use of arpeggios to flex the vocal cords or the French 'mask-emphasis', Grace Richards featured the *Embouchure* so familiar to wood-wind instrumentalists.

But, as I mentioned at the beginning, the

12

right mood of approach is of cardinal importance at the outset of this training.

First of all, one must find the calm to enter into a new dimension of reverent receptivity in order to experience the universal tone. Grace Richards used to repeat, *"Erwartungsvoller Ruhe"* —expectant calm. "Try not to try," she often said. The over-intensity that accompanies "trying hard" sets up tension in the vocal instrument, which blocks the free flowing of the tone. Naturally, the physical body, as the singer's instrument, must be accorded due consideration. To further relaxation, the student could begin this singing training in a sitting position, comfortably erect, and do a few deep-breathing exercises. An exacting ear training is of the essence. This should lead to the ability to hear with accuracy and discrimination the nuances of the teacher's illustrations as well as to judge properly one's own attempts. A teacher's vocal illustrations are indispensable for teaching this method. Unlike other methods in which the tone production comes first and the speech sounds follow, the pupil is asked instead to concentrate upon the initial consonant which, properly centered, provides the 'house', the shape within which the vowel is intoned on the desired pitch.

13

The centering or focusing of the tone is achieved through an articulated *Embouchure*. A flute player finds an *Embouchure* essential —so likewise a singer. This is by far the most unique and vital aspect of the method. One trains this *Embouchure* by means of pictures.

Visualize a tiny spot or aperture localized at the midpoint of the lower lip. On this imaginary pinpoint, the word is spoken in an unforced manner, centered and concentrated. One imagines the lower lip slightly drawn in, like that of a fish taking in air bubbles (this is only a preliminary step, and it cannot be too strongly emphasized that, in performing, the lips are not pursed in this way). The breath in the singer's mouth comes in contact with the outside air around the lips. The outside air, molded by the properly formed, articulated speech sound, acts like a sounding board or acoustical shell for all the resonators of head, nose, chest, mouth, and so forth; in short, of the entire vocal instrument, thereby giving the voice a free, full, ringing quality. The vibration thus set in motion comes about through the interplay of the universal tone and the singer, not by a forced physical effort. An indication that this is achieved will be the feeling that the lips and all the resonators vibrate of their own accord.

The inside and outside air then maintain a balanced interchange through the *Embouchure*. This balance is called the focus, and is the seed-center which produces the freely floating, round, ringing etheric tone. Such a tone can be enlarged just by letting more breath flow out, as the circles in a pond grow larger when a pebble is thrown into it.

A focused word on the desired pitch is thus the crux of this method here set forth so briefly, and its lofty goal is the marrying of speech and tone—needless to say, a lifetime study.

—Theodora Richards

III. TOWARD FREEDOM AND JOY IN SINGING

The importance of singing as a health-giving activity is becoming increasingly recognized. People sense that there is more to singing than the pleasant feeling one gets from it. Yet I have often heard the comment: "You know, I would very much like to sing, but I'm afraid I have no talent." Or "I would like to sing, but I can't carry a tune." It seems very sad indeed that the very people who would enjoy the activity, and might benefit from it most, do not feel they can even participate in a singing group. These individuals are almost always mistaken. In truth, everyone should sing, even those who think they cannot — in fact, *especially* those who think they cannot, because these are just the people, who, by using a right approach to singing, could free themselves both in the realm of singing and in other aspects of their lives as well.

Nowadays, we are beset by so many tensions that it is almost necessary to make our way back consciously to a 'natural' approach to singing. To some degree, learning how to sing is not so much a matter of learning what to do, as learning what *not* to do.

17

At an exhibition of Rodin's work, an elderly lady, who greatly admired his work, said to the sculptor: "But I do not see how you can possibly carve such a beautiful figure out of a shapeless block of marble!" To which Rodin replied: "Madame, it is very easy. The figure is there. All you need to do is cut away the unnecessary parts." This can also be said of singing. Learning to sing consciously is finding the inner coordination and balance which are necessary to allow tones to sing themselves. It is learning to discard obstructing elements which prevent a freely flowing tone. It is, in fact, learning not so much how to *make* things happen, as how to *allow* certain processes to occur. This is the task. Gracia Ricardo, an American singer active in the early years of this century, expressed it well when she said, you must "try not to try."

In looking at the professional singing world, one finds many references among singers and singing teachers to the "free voice," or the "natural voice." One hears people talk about such things as "placing the voice" and "breath support." One also sees, in many modern approaches to the study of voice, very detailed charts of the "singing organs": the larynx, the diaphragm, and the lungs. With these charts, many teachers try to teach their pupils how to sing. If students exposed to this latter method *do* learn how to sing, it is more than likely *in spite of* this approach than because of it. The truth is that, often, many students are ruined for life by such methods, and are made so conscious of the vocal organs and apparatus that they can hardly produce a free and joyous sound again, unless they find a way to unlearn the unfortunate results of these approaches. Despite all the obstacles, beautiful voices do, however, emerge—there is no doubt. Many finally come through by 'teaching themselves.' Birgit Nilsson, the famous Swedish soprano who is still producing glorious tones in her mid-sixties, is said to have been totally disillusioned with her singing teachers, and completely desperate, when she experimented on her own with a few high 'yelps' and "found her own voice." This method is not recommended for anyone without Miss Nilsson's experience. Yelping may be hazardous to your singing health.

Stuart Burrows is another extraordinary example. Although he possesses one of the most beautiful tenor voices today, he never took formal singing lessons. In general, the teachers who tamper the least with the vocal apparatus of their gifted pupils are the most successful. Some know instinctively what not to do and how to lead a talented singer to his or her own true and free voice. Of course, it is not enough to know what we should not do; we also need to know what positive actions we must take in order to sing. We have to know what will set the process going, what can help.

In her excellent article, *The Singer As Instrument*, part II of this publication, Theodora Richards suggests some of the things one can do, describing several steps which she developed based on study with her aunt, Gracia Ricardo. "First of all," she writes, "one must find the calm to enter into a new dimension of reverent receptivity in order to experience the 'universal tone'." She speaks of her aunt's repeated comment *"Erwartungsvolle Ruhe"* — expectant calm, as a basis for singing.

One of the most helpful suggestions in that article is the description of the *Embouchure,* which is a centering or focusing of the tone at an imaginary point of the lower lip. If done correctly in an unforced well-formed manner through an articulated speech sound, this will give the voice a free, ringing quality. The *Embouchure* approach makes full use of the resonances of the head without physically locking the tone into any one of the different resonators: nasal cavity, hard or soft palate, pharynx, or throat. To my knowledge, this is the first time that the *Embouchure* idea has been described in this way. Yet, when it is used, it does indeed help to bring about a free, ringing tone which, at the same time, provides a basis for the tones that will follow. As one soars and as one descends, provided

the rest of the instrument (the body) is pliant
and balanced, it offers a flexible anchor for
the full range of the singing voice.

Breathing, Coordination, Tone

"How do you breathe to sing?" someone
once asked Rudolf Steiner. "You breathe," he
said, somewhat wryly,[3] then making it clear
that the diaphragm must be involved. He
even suggested that the teacher place his
hand on the pupil's diaphragm to see if it
were, in fact, working properly. The question
comes back again and again: "How do you
breathe for singing?"

Nowadays, more than ever before, stress
and the general pace of life contribute to our
breathing very superficially — only with the
upper part of the lungs. This makes for strain
and tension in the voice. We have lost that
inner serenity which allows for a natural
deep breathing. And so we must reacquire it.
When breathing, one should feel that the
bottom of the lungs is also being filled with
breath. Observe how you breathe while you
are lying in bed, and about to fall asleep, or
when you awaken in the morning. You will
notice the natural rise and fall of the diaphragm and even of the abdomen. When
you are in an upright position, the same

breathing activity should be at work. (You can place your hand on your diaphragm to see if this is actually happening.) Sometimes it helps to think of breathing in through the soles of the feet. By means of certain exercises one can achieve the healing, natural coordination and balance in breathing which leads to an ever greater freedom in singing.

Although deep breathing is necessary for good singing, it is by no means sufficient. All the breathing exercises in the world will not assure good 'tone production'. No matter how developed the breathing becomes, we shall still not be able to make the transition from breathing well to singing well unless we learn how to 'breathe artistically' in conjunction with singing. Having understood this, we must realize that it is not so much a question of how much breath one has but rather how it is used. It is not so much the capacity, but the intensity of the breath that is necessary for tone. *Capacity* of breath can be achieved through breathing exercises alone, but the *intensity* of breath can only be achieved through exercises together with singing. High superficial breathing, Olga Hensel points out, cannot achieve this intensity.[4] Indeed, people who have such superficial breathing do not even experience movement in the area of the diaphragm when they breathe.

The tone has a life of its own. It is a spiritual essence. It comes through the body, not from it. It is as if a Being offered it to us, and we draw it in. It resounds through us, if the body is pliant and ready. With each note, a number of subtle adjustments will take place—even in the throat. The singer must not *make* these adjustments, but must *allow* them to happen. It is as if each tone were a child which is born into the world through us when we sing. If we are too tight, we hinder the tone—it will come out forced or pinched; if we are too relaxed, the tone will be faulty, breathy, or off pitch. The proper balance alone will allow the tone to emerge freely. The aim is to learn what the tone wants of us and to allow the natural coordinated movements to come about which will allow the tone to enter. In this way, one learns what is meant by the seeming paradox: Singing is a balanced combination of freedom and restraint.

In this process, balance, coordination, and all that is acquired in singing often begin to manifest in other aspects of one's life. When one sings in the right way, the whole person is actively engaged and the feeling is one of wholesomeness, balance, integration, and of being in command of one's self.

A Journey

Singing is a journey which pupil and teacher take together. A journey in which the student discovers unexplored spaces within and around him. Rudolf Steiner has described the singer's experience in terms of learning to find what "the air in him and around him is doing in its movement."[5] Tone is not air. Its essence has in fact nothing to do with the air. Air is a necessary conduit (or carrier) for the tone but is not the tone itself. When we sing, we transform breath into tone. Rudolf Steiner tells us that air is for the tone what the ground is for the person who stands upon it. The tone needs the air for support. "Tone itself, however, is something spiritual."[6] When we sing, we activate the air around us. Singing is movement. When tone resounds, forms are also created in and around us. When we sing together, forms are created between us. Singing is almost always an exciting journey, rich in self-discovery of various kinds. One can hardly make the journey without returning with some nuggets of self-knowledge as well.

Fear of Singing

As Hilda Deighton and Gina Palermo pointed out in their unpublished manuscript on the singing technique of Gracia Ricardo: "Each voice is unique and is a reflection of the inner being." They mention that Socrates said, "Let me hear his voice that I may know him."** One often encounters a reluctance to sing for fear that, in doing so, one will reveal too much of oneself. Yet, in spite of this fear, the desire to sing is there. This fear can gradually be overcome by approaching the singing in a particular way — usually with a teacher in a kind of conversation in tone. At first, the student always sings in unison with another voice, then gradually gains the courage to sing a few tones on his own. Fear gradually diminishes as he realizes that this is a path he can follow. The more one can immerse oneself in the music or simply in the tone or interval, the more one can forget oneself in the process, and a step in freedom is achieved. As a child learns to walk, so can some adults learn to sing.

**Socrates was (most likely) referring to the speaking voice, but these words are just as true — perhaps more so — for the singing voice.

Singing Off Pitch

The question concerning the inability to sing on pitch requires a meditative approach. One must listen very carefully to a tone — then immerse oneself in it, become *one* with it, so to speak. When fully within the experience of that tone, one joins or blends with it. As Rudolf Steiner points out, the ear and larynx must be considered together for they form a totality.[7] They cannot be separated from each other in one's understanding of singing and speech, nor even in physiology. Sometimes, the work requires infinite patience, but it is always worth the effort. If the problem is severe, the only way to deal with it is in private sessions with a teacher. As the singer becomes stronger and more confident, he or she can return as a real asset to the group. Imagine the experience of being able to match in pitch what you hear, when you thought you could not trust yourself to do this. A student once said, "The most important thing I have learned from my singing lessons is how to listen." And, she might have added, "how to coordinate what I hear with what I sing." The words of Rudolf Steiner: "Ear and larynx form a totality," become a matter of one's own experience. The above-mentioned singer was unable at the outset to distinguish one tone from another in pitch, but learned through her lessons to sing rather difficult intervals and simple songs with ease. An enormous sense of confidence was the result.

Rudolf Steiner and Singing

Among some of the very interesting references Rudolf Steiner makes to singing is the comment: "The singer must acquire a consciousness not so much for the motion of his own physical organs as for what the air does in its movement in and around him." He speaks of "leading the tone over into the etheric."[8] One begins to sense the meaning of these words when a tone which a student has sung is heard reverberating from elsewhere in the room — or 'shimmering' in the air around one.

Singers have told me that they "feel" certain tones somewhere *above* the head, like a sparkling "point," or elsewhere around the head. If one feels the tone in the throat in an uncomfortable way, or with any sense of pressure, it is not free. One should stop immediately and seek another approach. Sometimes *movement* — eurythmy gestures are often best — can help free a person from physical tensions as a prelude to singing.

Several students of Rudolf Steiner who worked intensively with Anthroposophy have contributed interesting and helpful insights into the question of liberating the tone. The above-mentioned Gracia Ricardo, her niece, Theodora Richards, Maria Fuehrmann,[9] Olga Hensel, Madame Werbeck-Svärdström, her devoted pupil, Juergen Schriefer, and Karl Gerbert[10] are some of the dedicated 'seekers after truth' in the realm of singing.

Madame Werbeck-Svärdström titled her book *Uncovering the Voice*. This image is quite a true one. The voice must be uncovered, even *dis*covered, in each of us. When a beautiful voice emerges, it is not that it was 'created' by the teacher. No teacher can *make* a beautiful voice. But a teacher can help remove all that which stands in the way of true tone, and can thus help make a voice beautiful—much like the uncovering of a diamond. It is sometimes a true source of wonder where diamonds lie hidden.

I remember in particular the uncovering of one sparkling gem, where no indication of such an instrument was there to begin with. Such an experience fills one with wonder and gratitude.

28

Sometimes our sense of tonal memory must also be discovered. This requires patience, extreme concentration, intensive listening, matching of tones. But organs of tonal perception can also be developed and, in so doing, one opens up many other faculties of hearing and perception which were not available to us before. It is a discovery on many more levels than one at first realizes.

Singing with Children

Singing for and with children requires a particular kind of approach. Here, an easy, flowing sound is imperative. Easy, not in the pop singer sense, but in a pure, unforced, pleasant way and, above all, joyful. For little children, the sound must be joyful, not somber. It must be pure—pure, above all, of adult emotions. If one chooses the right songs and sings them simply, giving attention to the mood of the song, the songs will sing themselves in the right way.

The choosing of songs for children is in itself an art. What is right for the child at a particular age is a study worth undertaking, if one is to do justice to one's job as a teacher and as a parent. Rudolf Steiner, in his suggested curriculum for Waldorf teachers, has given many indications concerning the type of music and songs which are appropriate for the child at various stages of his development.[11] For instance, Dr. Steiner tells us that, up to the age of nine, the child lives primarily in the mood of the fifth. Pentatonic songs reflecting this mood are, for the most part, the ones that should be sung with the children until the ninth year.[12] From the tenth to the twelfth year, the child should be brought to the experience of the major and minor thirds beginning with simple two-part rounds. Care should be taken, however, that each part is learned well before the two parts are put together. Later, two-part songs may be taken. As the child grows, three-part rounds of increasing difficulty can be added, as well as folk songs which can be sung by children of all ages, but which should be carefully chosen to suit the different ages. At age twelve, the experience of the octave should be brought in. Songs with octave leaps can now be given. Mozart, Beethoven and Bach can be introduced to the child of thirteen and fourteen either in unison with accompaniment, or in parts of varying degrees of complexity, depending on the musical ability of the class. Through such works, they can be lead to appreciate the beauty of music. And what they sing should be "well sung" according to Rudolf Steiner's suggestions.

He points to the importance not only of choosing the right songs but also of singing well for the children. Children cannot be 'taught' to sing in the same way as adults. As you sing, so will they. If you are free and joyful in your singing, they will be also. If you are fearful, out of tune, breathy, or cloudy in your singing, chances are that the children through their natural predisposition for imitation will pick up at least some if not all of these characteristics. It is, in fact, as important to sing well for the children as it is to speak well for them. Sloppy speech, where one can hardly make out the words spoken, is harmful to the formative speech organs of the child; sloppy and careless singing, especially with regard to intonation, is also harmful. The inner ear of the child cannot but be damaged by inaccurately sung tones. Whether you sing pentatonic songs, simple folk songs, or even one or two intervals, the intonation should be completely accurate. In music, to be almost on pitch is not enough. If a teacher has difficulties singing simple songs on pitch, then either the teacher is not listening attentively enough to the tones he is singing or he is having vocal problems which are preventing the necessary freedom that allows the tones to be naturally on pitch. It is important that teachers take the time and effort to learn to sing as well as they can, so that ease and joy, but also accuracy, can prevail in the sound.

Olga Hensel, who studied singing in the light of anthroposophical thought, pointed out in her book *Die Geistige Grundlage des Gesanges (The Spiritual Basis of Singing)* that the use of the "full-blown" voice, which describes the fullest emotions of the human being in passionate song, is tactless when singing for children. Children do not yet have the faculties to comprehend these emotions. This is why they sometimes make fun of the singers. It is their way of shrugging off something which is totally foreign to them, which is, in fact, too much for them to absorb.

Is Singing For Everyone?

No! If, by singing, one means a glorious voice and a professional career. *Yes!* If, by singing, we mean joyful, healthy song which lifts the spirit and brings people together in a community of sound. If everyone would sing in Congress before the day began; if teachers would gather for a song at the start of the day; if factory workers would do the same, interweaving their tones into the spaces between them for fifteen minutes, and then go about their day's work, it would introduce an element into daily life which would foster healthy, social feelings in a simple and unaffected way.

Singing is a creative activity which, when done with others, brings about a harmony, unforced and joyous. It is hard to dislike another person when you are singing with him or her. It is as if a higher being descended into your midst to make peace during those moments and, whatever may have occurred before, whatever may occur later, in that moment, our souls vibrate in unison. Given enough such moments, we may gradually wear down the barriers of hatred, of envy, of discontent. When we sing together as a group, these feelings have no place. The heart warms when people sing together.

I remember an incident in which two teachers had quarrelled just before a rehearsal. The atmosphere was heavy with irritation, even anger. The rehearsal began and, as we all sang, something seemed to dissolve all those negative feelings. It was as if an aura of forgiveness had taken their place. Everything else just seemed unimportant. What wondrous thing is this that can happen when people make music together, especially when they sing? It was as if the singing could unite souls, could dissolve irritation and impatience—could, in fact, heal souls. Singing can have a healing effect on our personalities and help us to attain a feeling of wholeness. Done rightly, it is, of course, also a skill which will enable us to sing songs well, clearly, on pitch, and with a pleasant sound.

Important, too, is the fact that if we have achieved the proper freedom, this wholeness will communicate itself to the listener as well, and will have a healing effect there, too.

Correct singing helps lead one to an awareness of inner coordination, inner balances, the inner and outer world of tone, the connection of the upper and lower — the heights and the depths in one's own being. Singing is such an intimate matter, bound up with one of the most intimate aspects of ourselves—the voice—that one can hardly enter this realm without touching upon the deepest realities. It is almost a holy path. The student does well to take care that it be trodden only with those who are aware that the task goes far beyond the mechanistic and materialistic.

Singing enriches, ennobles and strengthens the soul and contributes in large measure to the search for one's own sense of self in its highest form. Yet, when all is said and done, it is also the simplest form of joy that one can experience.

—Dina Soresi Winter

NOTES

[1] See Footnote on page 3.
[2] See Footnote on page 5.

[3] From conversations with Olga Hensel, author of *Die Geistige Grundlage des Gesanges*, in Stuttgart, and from Hilda Deighton and Gina Palermo's as yet unpublished manuscript on the singing technique of Gracia Ricardo.

[4] Olga Hensel: *Die Geistige Grundlage des Gesanges (The Spiritual Basis of Singing)*, Stuttgart, Baerenreiter Verlag, 1952. Not available in English.

[5] Rudolf Steiner, *Wege der Geistigen Erkenntnis und der Erneuerung Kuenstlerischer Weltenschauung*, Dornach, Rudolf Steiner Verlag, 1980 (GA 161). Lecture 1, January 1, 1915, *(Paths to Spiritual Knowledge and to the Renewal of the Artistic World View)*; not yet published in English.

[6] Rudolf Steiner, *The Inner Nature of Music and the Experience of Tone*, Lecture IV, December 2, 1922, Spring Valley, Anthroposophic Press, 1983.

[7] Rudolf Steiner *The Light Course* (First Scientific Lecture Course), Lecture 8, December 31, 1919, Forest Row, Sussex, Steiner Schools Fellowship, 1977. Translated by George Adams.

[8] Rudolf Steiner, *Wege der Geistigen Erkenntnis und der Erneuerung Kuenstlerischer Weltenschauung (Paths to Spiritual Knowledge and to the Renewal of the Artistic World)*; not yet published in English.

[9] Maria Führmann wrote *Die Praxis des Gesanges unter geisteswissenschaftlichen Gesichtspunkt (The Practice of Singing in the Light of Spiritual Science)*, Freiburg, i. Br. Verlag Die Kommenden, 1959. Not available in English. This study includes a description of the connection between planets and tone. Her book is greatly influenced by the research of Anny von Lange.

[10] Karl Gerbert wrote a pamphlet called *Das ABC der Stimmbildung (The ABC of Voice Development)*, Stuttgart: Verlag Freies Geistesleben, 1970. Not available in English.

[11] *Rudolf Steiner's Curriculum for Waldorf Schools* by E.A. Karl Stockmeyer and *Curriculum of the First Waldorf School* assembled by Caroline von Heydebrand, translated and with additional notes by Eileen Hutchins. Forest Row,

Sussex, Steiner Schools Fellowship, 1982 and 1984 respectively.

[12] Among other studies, the work of Elisabeth Lebret is most helpful for children up to the ninth year. See: *The Shepherd's Songbook* for grades I, II and III of Waldorf Schools. Private Edition, 1975; and the booklet *Pentatonic Songs for Nursery and Kindergarten and Grades 1 and 2*.